WINGS OVER WASHINGTON

BY DAVID G GORDON

Edited by Teresa Roupe.

Design by Brookie Branch.

Copyedited by Carey Vendrame.

Typesetting by Graphic Traffic, Santa Barbara, CA.

Produced by Sequoia Communications
2020 Alameda Padre Serra
Santa Barbara, CA 93103 (805) 963-9336
Printed in Hong Kong
ISBN 0-917859-97-9
First Printing, 1989

SEQUOIA
COMMUNICATIONS

Special thanks to the following people for their contribution to this book: Howard Lovering, Ralph Johnston, and Anne Rutledge at the Museum of Flight; Paul Spitzer, Bill Jury and Marilyn Phipps at the Boeing Company; Peter M. Bowers; Bob Moody from the North Cascades Smoke Jumper Base; Captain Gene Davis at the Coast Guard Museum; Ann McCreary in Engineering Publications and Professor Kristina B. Katsaros, Department of Atmospheric Sciences at the University of Washington; Hal Alabaster at the National Oceanic and Atmospheric Administration; and Don Wilson at the Port of Seattle.

Photo on page 3: Pilot Maude McClaine.

The author gratefully acknowledges Linda Lewis for her major contribution to the research and writing of this book.

P H O T O   C R E D I T S

DANIEL B. ALLISON COLLECTION: 19 bottom. THE BOEING COMPANY ARCHIVE: 2, 4, 11 middle, 12, 13 top left, top right and bottom, 14-15 5th from left and far right, 18 top, 22 left and bottom right, 23, 32 left and right, 33, 34-35 5th from left, 41 top, 43 inset, 44-45 4th and 6th from left, 47. PETER BOWERS COLLECTION: 19 middle, 30 top, 34-35 far left top, 37 right. CLARA BROWNE COLLECTION: 28 left, 29 bottom right. CARL CLEVELAND: 16. CHRIS EDEN: 46 top. JOHN FERGUSON: outside front flap. MONTANA HISTORICAL SOCIETY: 11 top. MUSEUM OF FLIGHT ARCHIVE: 3, 11 bottom, 14-15 2nd from left, 20 left, middle and right, 29 top right, 31 top, 34-35 far left bottom, 37 left, 42, 44-45 5th from left. NASA: 44-45 far left bottom. NOAA: 40. NORTH CASCADES SMOKE JUMPER BASE: 36 top and bottom. HENRY PAYLOR COLLECTION: 26. PORT OF SEATTLE: 43, 44-45 far left top, 3rd from left, and far right. JOEL ROGERS: 46 bottom. SEA-TAC AIRPORT: 24, 25. VICTOR SEELY: 34-35 6th from left. SMITHSONIAN INSTITUTION ARCHIVE: 9. EVERETT E. SOLDIN: 14-15 4th from left. UNITED AIRLINES: 18 bottom, 19 top, 21 background and right, 22 top right, 34-35 far right and 3rd from left. UNIVERSITY OF WASHINGTON COLLECTION: 1, 6, 8, 10 left and right, 14-15 far left and 3rd from left, 41 bottom left and bottom right. U.S. DEPT. OF AGRICULTURE: 38. U.S. NAVY: 27 top right. ART WALKER COLLECTION: 30 bottom left, 34-35 4th from left. JACK R. WHITNALL COLLECTION: 36 background. GORDON S. WILLIAMS COLLECTION: 27 background, top left, middle, 28 right, 31 bottom.

I L L U S T R A T I O N   C R E D I T S

Brookie Branch: cover, inside back cover. Erin Reinecke Balint: page 3, hand-coloring.

TABLE OF CONTENTS

It Began With a Balloon

ONE

The Alaska-Yukon-Pacific Exposition

Glimpsed from the air, the ornate, palatial architecture, formal gardens, and broad walkways of the Alaska-Yukon-Pacific Exposition of 1909 radiated outward from a central fountain like the spokes of a great wheel.

Those that could not savor the scenery from the 68-foot dirigible hovering high above Seattle's turn-of-the-century celebration were more than content to catch a peek of the airship as it passed overhead. Designed by F.C. Dittman and piloted by amateur aerialist J.C. "Bud" Mars, the spectacular hydrogen-filled bag delighted hundreds of fairgoers during the first five days of the event.

Souvenir snapshots of the Alaska-Yukon-Pacific Exposition grounds taken from a much smaller balloon were also popular that year. According to photographer Richard T. Jones, hundreds of his well-received prints were made from only two negatives. His were the first aerial photographs of any part of Seattle—and, for that matter, any part of the state.

Clearly, the popularity of Dittman's dirigible and Jones' pictures offered early proof of Washington's love affair with flight. In the years to come, the relationship would blossom.

Aviation and aerospace technology have grown to become an integral part of our state. To understand the true origins of this phenomenon, we must first turn the hands of time back 20 years before the A-Y-P Exposition, and look at the achievements of Washington's hot air and hydrogen balloonists. Could these brave souls have possibly imagined what would rise up over the years in the wake of their early aircraft?

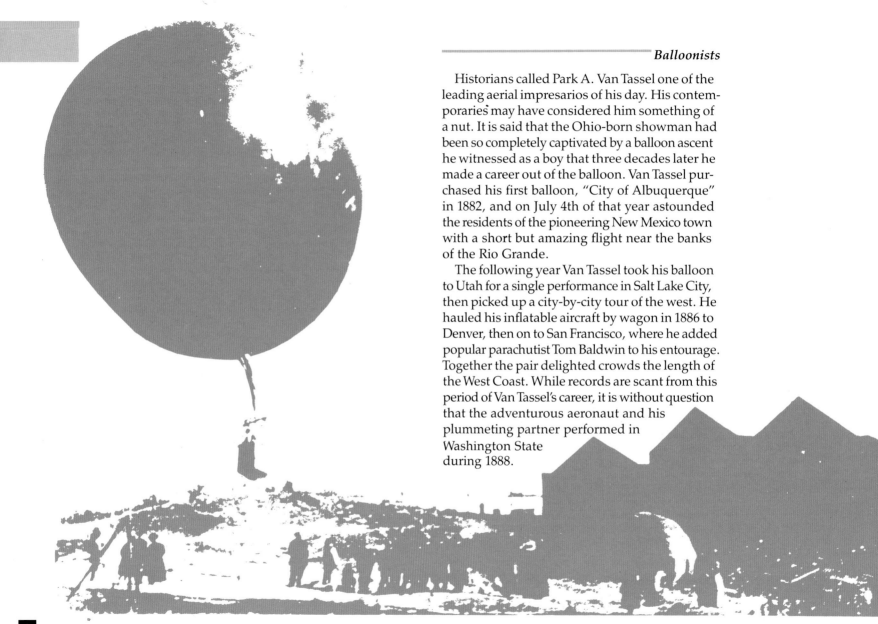

Historians called Park A. Van Tassel one of the leading aerial impresarios of his day. His contemporaries may have considered him something of a nut. It is said that the Ohio-born showman had been so completely captivated by a balloon ascent he witnessed as a boy that three decades later he made a career out of the balloon. Van Tassel purchased his first balloon, "City of Albuquerque" in 1882, and on July 4th of that year astounded the residents of the pioneering New Mexico town with a short but amazing flight near the banks of the Rio Grande.

The following year Van Tassel took his balloon to Utah for a single performance in Salt Lake City, then picked up a city-by-city tour of the west. He hauled his inflatable aircraft by wagon in 1886 to Denver, then on to San Francisco, where he added popular parachutist Tom Baldwin to his entourage. Together the pair delighted crowds the length of the West Coast. While records are scant from this period of Van Tassel's career, it is without question that the adventurous aeronaut and his plummeting partner performed in Washington State during 1888.

Balloonist Park A. Van Tassel.

Washington's first native-born aeronaut was the "Wild Scotsman," L. Guy Mecklem. In fact, Washingtonians have been hard pressed to find a more crazed or colorful hero since. Mecklem first took to the sky as a 15-year-old working in the boat house of Seattle's Leschi Park, plunging from a hot air balloon into the cold waters of Lake Washington in 1897. His initial flight was one of the attractions of the Seattle Amusement Center, which later hired Mecklem to replace their original ailing balloonist. A career was launched.

Mecklem was later hired by realtor C.D. Hillman, who wanted to attract people to his latest Seattle development, Hillman City, near the south end of Lake Washington. The pay was exceptional—$150 per ascension and bail-out—and Mecklem was quick to establish a reputation as Washington's premiere aerial daredevil.

In 1907 Mecklem designed and built his own airship, a large, silken, elongated balloon 58 feet in length, that was powered by an air-cooled, two-cylinder Curtiss engine. The massive gasbag of his craft was inflated with air from a blacksmith's forge blower and was put in service during the summer of 1908 at Luna Park, a West Seattle waterfront attraction famous for its concessions, rides, and shows. That same year, Mecklem accepted the challenge to race his dirigible against two automobiles, covering a distance of ten miles between Luna Park and the Meadows, a horse racetrack that later became the site of Boeing Field. Mecklem beat his competitors to the finish line by a full two minutes. After the race, the Wild Scotsman retired his dirigible to a hangar, where he charged curious spectators ten cents each to see it.

Left: The "bird man," Charles Hamilton, takes time out to pose at the Meadows airstrip. Right: Hamilton's Curtiss biplane soared high over Seattle's Meadows Racetrack on March 11, 1910.

The Aero Club of the Northwest

It didn't take long for word of the Wright Brothers' 1903 accomplishments at Kitty Hawk, North Carolina, to capture the imagination of Washington's free-thinking fliers. However, it wasn't until 1910 that the first airplane actually appeared in the state, when Charles K. Hamilton brought down his yellow-winged Curtiss biplane at Seattle's Meadows Racetrack in front of thousands of curious onlookers.

Hamilton's appearance increased the enthusiasm of the state's aspiring aviators. One by one, daring Washingtonians earned their wings,

literally begging, borrowing, buying, or building whatever primitive aircraft they could. In 1915 William Boeing founded the Aero Club of the Northwest, a locally sanctioned branch of the Aero Club of America. He set up the club's headquarters in a seaplane hangar on Seattle's Lake Union and designed a pennant—one that depicted the club mascot, a mallard drake, in full flight. From its inception, the club boasted 19 charter members, several from the military, although Boeing and his associate Herb Munter were among a handful of Seattleites, licensed or unlicensed, who could truly call themselves pilots.

Above: Terah Maroney (on the right) is joined by Eddie Hubbard at the wheel of his 1915 seaplane.

HERB MUNTER can be credited with having built and flown the state's first airplane, a "flying crate" of wood and home-sewn fabric tied together with wire. Munter was 18 years old at the time. "We built the steering wheel and the seat first so we could 'hangar fly' on the ground when we became impatient at the length of time it was taking to complete the plane," he later explained. Four years later, while he was in the middle of building his fourth airplane, he was asked to become the first employee of the Boeing Airplane Company, which was then known as the Pacific Aero Products Company, in Seattle.

Below: A moment of terror frozen in time—J. Clifford Turpin plows into the Meadows grandstand.

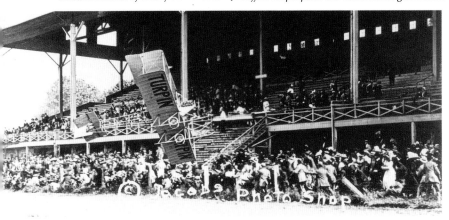

TERAH T. MARONEY moved from Montana to Washington in 1915 to operate a flying school in Seattle. It was here that he took Bill Boeing, a young lumber magnate, for his first airplane ride. The experience undoubtedly inspired the founder of the Boeing Airplane Company to add to his list of careers. Maroney's influence on Washington aviation history didn't stop there—he also flew with Eddie Hubbard, Herb Munter, and taught dozens of people to fly.

Below: Herb Munter (shown here in a Boeing Model C) built his first airplane at age 18.

J. CLIFFORD TURPIN, a graduate of the Wright School in Dayton, Ohio, was one of Washington's favorite exhibition pilots. Together with Phil O. Parmelee, a second out-of-state flier, he mesmerized crowds throughout the Northwest with his amazing aerial antics. The partnership, however, was short-lived. On May 29, 1912, in Seattle, Turpin lost control of his airplane, a Hall-Scott powered Gage tractor biplane, plowing into the Meadows grandstand. Although Turpin was unharmed, one person was killed and at least 20 others were injured. Parmelee crashed two days later, attempting to fly against strong, gusty winds at an engagement in Yakima. Turpin, who brought Parmelee's body back to his Michigan home, gave up flying forever.

Clairmont L. Egtvedt

CLAIRMONT L. EGTVEDT served as Boeing's chief engineer during the factory's formative years. He joined the company in 1917, a draftsman fresh from the University of Washington. He was able to convince William Boeing to enlarge his engineering staff, and during his prolific career as chief engineer, was responsible for the design of the PW-9, the Model 40, Model 80, and the development of the legendary B-17 "Flying Fortress." He would later become operations vice president, then president, and, in 1939, chairman of Boeing's board.

Boeing's First Airplanes

William Boeing was an easy victim of the fever to fly. Shortly after graduating from Glenn Martin's flying school in Santa Ana, California, the only son of a wealthy Midwest timberman plunked down $10,000 on a Martin TA seaplane, which he shipped to Seattle in October 1915. Floyd Smith, Boeing's flight instructor at the Martin School, was on hand at Lake Union to uncrate and assemble the airplane, as was Herb Munter, a young mechanic whom Boeing had hired to help fly his new two-seater.

Before the year was over, Munter would swim away from two crashes with the Martin. The following year Boeing would sell the seaplane and launch a totally new enterprise. His single goal: to build a better airplane.

Boeing joined forces with G. Conrad Westerveldt, an engineering officer in the U.S. Navy, to form what was then known as the Pacific Aero Products Company. First off the Boeing "assembly line" in May 1916 was a float-equipped biplane, the B & W, which was named after the company's two founders. One year later, the firm changed its name to the Boeing Airplane Company and unveiled the second in a long line of successful aircraft, the C series airplane.

By 1926 Boeing's "Red Barn" factory was operating at peak production. In 1928 the *Christian Science Monitor* called the Red Barn complex "the largest factory in the U.S. devoted exclusively to the manufacture of aircraft." But even the *Monitor* couldn't forecast the growth of the Boeing Airplane Company or its impact on the economy and overall complexion of Washington over the next 60 years.

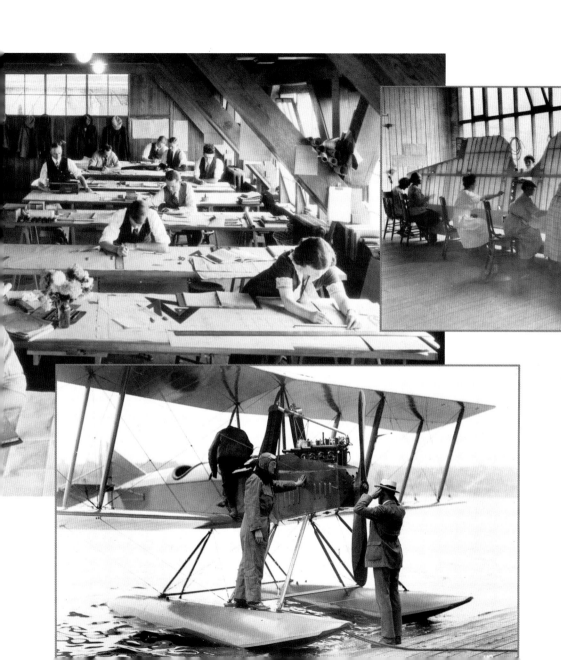

Above left: The Boeing Airplane Company's design office. Above right: Boeing Airplane Company workers originally sewed fabric wing covers by hand. Below left: William Boeing (poised on a pontoon) was a familiar figure at Lake Union's seaplane station.

Left to right: One dollar got you into Hamilton's extravaganza. • Daredevil Fred Wiseman's Curtiss Pusher visited Olympia in 1911. • Filling the great gasbag at the A-Y-P Exposition. • At first, Boeing's factory was also the Heath shipyard. • Team spirit helped Boeing's welded steel fuselage frame materialize. • A rarity—this C series trainer with single pontoon and floats.

FUSELAGE FRAME

Scrapbook

Aviation Comes of Age

TWO

Felts Field in 1929.

The Spokane Air Race of 1927

There wasn't much of Spokane that was visible from the air back in 1927, just the monolithic clocktower of the Great Northern Railroad station, rising up like a solitary sentinel. But you can bet that Nick Mamer saw even less of the city as he streaked across the Idaho border, completing the last leg of Spokane's National Air Races on September 24th of that year.

Seventy planes had entered the two races, which originated in both Los Angeles and New York and culminated in Spokane. Nearly 100,000 people bought tickets for the two days of record-breaking performances and heart-stopping acrobatics preceding the race. Each pilot hotly competed for $60,000 in prize money put up by the business community of Spokane. Mamer, flying his Wright J5-powered, open-cockpit biplane built specially for the event by the Buhl Aircraft Company, finished third in the Class A event.

Could Mamer or anyone who witnessed the race's exciting conclusion have guessed that they were rushing headlong into a new era of flight? The flying machine was rapidly gaining acceptance, and becoming an exciting, effective new mode of transportation instead of a novelty.

In less than two years, eastern and western Washington would have their first reliable air link, and by the end of the 1930s, air transportation would be an integral part of Washington life. The airplane would help turn the tide of World War II, and provide valuable services in the years of peace that followed.

Above: A Seattle office advertises carriers later
absorbed by United Air Lines.
Below: Leon Cuddeback and his Swallow mail airplane flew the first load of domestic contract mail

When it came to flying the mail, the peacetime service that got the nation's airline industry off the ground, Washington could claim three firsts:

• On March 3, 1919, Bill Boeing and Eddie Hubbard flew 60 letters from Vancouver to Seattle—a three-hour trip that included a refueling stop in Edmonds—and successfully completed the first North American international airmail flight in history.

• The next year, on October 15th, when Hubbard again loaded his airplane, a new B-1 Flying Boat, with letters and put five mail sacks aboard a Japanese transpacific liner in Victoria, British Columbia, he scored yet another first for the Evergreen State—the first regularly scheduled international airmail service—which he continued to operate until 1928.

• Seven years would pass before Washingtonians could claim their third airmail first. In 1926 the small eastern Washington town of Pasco would become the point of origin for the first official load of contract mail.

On April 6th of that year, 2,500 people gathered to watch Varney Air Line pilot Leon Cuddeback take off with 200 lbs. of mail and fly the desolate "nowhere route" between Pasco, Washington, and Elko, Nevada.

A second Varney pilot, Franklin Rose, was not so lucky. Returning from Elko, his Swallow bi-plane was blown off course. When it set down at the Idaho-Nevada border, it became mired in the mud. Rose had to hike to the nearest ranch, borrow a horse, and ride 30 miles to phone in his disastrous report.

Walter Varney

Walter Varney was a flier from San Mateo, California, who became a great promoter of airmail service in the Northwest. Despite a rather turbulent start, 90 percent of his Varney Air Line flights were completing their routes by the end of 1927. Varney had replaced his Swallows with Stearman C-3MBs, popular mail planes known for their reliability and ease of handling. He designed a one-ounce message sheet that he dubbed the "Air-O-Gram," and he persuaded many Northwest letter writers to use it.

In the summer of 1929 Varney won the route linking Portland, Seattle, and Spokane with Pasco. In the spring of 1930 he added passenger service on all routes.

Eddie Hubbard

Eddie Hubbard was one of the earliest and most effective advocates for flying the mail. In 1926 Hubbard persuaded Bill Boeing to set up Boeing Air Transport and to bid on the San Francisco-to-Chicago mail route. On January 15, 1927, Boeing Air Transport won the route with a scandalously low bid. Hubbard's competitors in the young industry were certain that Boeing would lose his shirt.

Boeing Air Transport started service on July 1, 1927, with a fleet of 25 new Boeing 40-A biplanes, specially designed for efficient cargo carrying. A new air-cooled engine, the Pratt and Whitney Wasp, could match the horsepower of the old Liberty-style engines while weighing less.

Soon it was apparent that Boeing Air Transport would not lose a cent. To Hubbard's delight, Bill Boeing thumbed his nose at all the doomsayers, adding that he, unlike the competition, "was in the business of carrying mail instead of radiators and water."

Vern Gorst

For Vern Gorst, a Port Orchard native, transportation meant airplanes. Shortly after Walter Varney made Pasco an air link, Gorst brought commercial airmail service to Seattle, forming Pacific Air Transport in 1925 and bidding on the Los Angeles-to-Seattle route.

In 1928 Boeing Air Transport bought Pacific Air Transport. Gorst used his share of the profits to acquire a B-1D flying boat, with which he introduced air service from Seattle to Alaska. Later, along with Percy Barnes, he took over Eddie Hubbard's Seattle-to-Victoria mail run. He also started Seattle Flying Service, added an air ferry between Seattle and Bremerton, and built the world's first floating hangar on Seattle's Lake Union.

Above left: Walter Varney (center), flanked by his wife and father, pioneered private domestic airmail service. Above right: Eddie Hubbard sold this Fokker Universal to Pacific Air Transport in 1927. Below: Vern Gorst, his son in his arms, poses with his family.

Air Routes

By 1929 airmail routes linked the state and tied the whole country together. As the nation grew closer, certain companies grew larger. The government, in the way it granted airmail contracts, seemed to encourage this all-encompassing trend. A myriad of small airfields sprung up on both sides of the Cascade Mountains to serve the carriers of Washington's mail.

Late in 1928 a company called United Aircraft & Transport Corporation came into being. It took in Boeing Airplane Company, Pratt & Whitney, Chance Vought, the Hamilton Propeller Company, Boeing Air Transport, and Pacific Air Transport. Bill Boeing was chairman of the board. This was the largest organization of its kind in the country, and still growing. On May 7, 1930, after several years of negotiations, United Aircraft & Transport acquired National Air Transport, the carrier flying the Chicago-to-New York route. The four airlines in the conglomerate operated as United Air Lines, the first coast-to-coast carrier and the largest air transport organization in the nation. Phil Johnson was president.

In 1934, a presidential order changed commercial aviation forever. Trust-buster Franklin Roosevelt cancelled all the private airmail contracts and split up the big aeronautical firms. The Boeing Airplane Company was on its own once again, forcibly split off from the rest of the conglomerate. A disgusted Bill Boeing sold out his interest and never again was involved in aviation, while Phil Johnson moved north to Canada and helped establish Trans-Canada Airlines.

Background: Pasco was the starting point for airmail's "nowhere route."

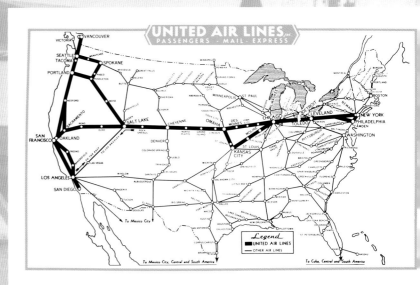

By 1934, United, the first coast-to-coast carrier, was the largest airline in the nation.

A Precious Cargo: Passengers

With the airmail gravy gone, passengers became Washington's most prized cargo. From the beginning of private airmail routes, people had ridden along with the mail bags. However, the number of courageous souls interested in riding in cold and uncomfortable quarters was limited; in 1926, for example, all the airlines in the country had carried a total of only 5,782 passengers.

The knowledge that thousands of mail sacks were getting to their destinations unscathed encouraged Washingtonians to take to the air. Boeing Airplane Company airplanes, more reliable than earlier airplanes and increasingly more comfortable, helped attract passengers. After its dependable 40-A, Boeing introduced the 40B-4, which could carry four passengers, had heat in its cabin, and a hinged table that could fold down from the forward bulkhead. It could travel at 125 mph, and, conditions permitting, could make the transcontinental trip in 31 hours and 45 minutes.

Boeing's next great advance in passenger com-

Above left: Registered nurses were the original stewardesses, introduced in 1930 on Boeing Air Transport airplanes. Above right: The "Flying Pullman," Boeing's Model 80-A, carried passengers coast-to-coast. Right: Valeria Tucker was the first stewardess on Boeing's Los Angeles to Seattle route.

fort and safety was the Model 80, affectionately known as the "Flying Pullman." This trimotored biplane cruised at 115 mph transporting up to 12 passengers in unrivaled luxury. It had forced-air heating, hot and cold running water, leather upholstery, individual reading lights, and a lavatory. A coast-to-coast flight aboard the 1928 Model 80 took 27 hours and 45 minutes and cost $259.50 per person.

Boeing Air Transport led the pack in developing passenger service. In 1929 a total of 6,129 people flew in and out of Chicago on Boeing air planes. Closer to home, Vern Gorst's Seattle-Bremerton Air Ferry set a record that same year by carrying 10,000 passengers in 90 days.

On May 15, 1930, Boeing Air Transport scored another first, adding a further refinement—eight registered nurses called stewardesses—to its San Francisco-to-Chicago flight. These original flight attendants poured coffee from a silver service, dished up creamed chicken from a thermos and attended to passengers' needs throughout the flight.

On February 8, 1933, Boeing took its Model 247, the prototype for the modern airliner, out for its first test flight. Not only could the two-engine monoplane cruise at a speed of 160 mph, it was also the first aircraft featuring retractable landing gear, deicer boots on wings and tail, supercharged engines, and controllable pitch propellers. As this magnificent ship lifted off Boeing Field and soared out over Puget Sound, Boeing engineer Monty Monteith was heard to exclaim, "They'll never build 'em any bigger." United Air Lines bought 60 of these sophisticated flyers and pressed them immediately into service.

Thorp Hiscock

Mail sacks weren't afraid of anything, but passengers wanted safety first. This strong desire prompted changes in the way airplanes flew. One innovative Washingtonian was responsible for many of the inventions that greatly reduced the risks of flying.

Thorp Hiscock was an electronics wizard who lived on a Yakima ranch. He was also Bill Boeing's brother-in-law, a fortunate circumstance that helped him enter and improve the electronic era of flying.

Among Hiscock's impressive credits:
- the two-way radio for ground-to-air communication
- the first successful automatic pilot
- the first practical set of wing deicers
- a device for changing the propeller pitch once the airplane gained altitude
- a device to control the temperature of the fuel while the airplane was in flight

The term "air port" was born in 1926, when the first federal air regulations were passed. Spokane's Felts Field was one of the first landing strips in the country to have this official designation bestowed upon it.

In the years preceding federal control, most airplanes touched down on dirt and sand strips, in grain fields or pastures—even on golf courses. Renton acquired one of the first manicured air strips in the state, when, in the summer of 1922, the delta at Bryn Mawr was leveled off, hay was cut, and a 2,300-foot dirt and sand runway was packed down.

Gorst Field, "the old sand lot," served as Seattle's only commercial field from 1926 to 1928. Its 1,800-foot runway was made out of gravel and clinkers spread evenly over soft sand, and covered with a layer of sawdust (which in winter tended to float on top of the field's numerous puddles). Gorst gave way to Boeing Field, which was informally opened on July 7, 1928, by Sally "The Lady with the Fan" Rand, who flew in from Portland, Oregon, for her date at Seattle's Fifth Avenue Theater. The actual dedication took place 19 days later in front of an appreciative crowd of 40,000 well wishers.

A highlight of 1935 at the Bryn Mawr/Renton airport was the stopover internationally renowned aviator Wiley Post and entertainer Will Rogers made on their attempted around-the-world flight.

Seattle-Tacoma International Airport took over most of the state's passenger traffic in the 1950s.

Their Lockheed Orion/Explorer had its wheels removed and pontoons installed by a Bryn Mawr crew, and on August 7th a huge crowd turned out to watch the pair fly north to Alaska. This was one of the last pit stops either flier would make; eight days later both men were killed when their airplane crashed on the tundra near Point Barrow.

The 1940s heralded a period of rapid expansion throughout Washington, due primarily to the efforts of the Works Progress Administration (WPA), and military readiness for World War II. Whatcom County Airport got a paved runway in 1940, and Everett received Paine Field—both projects courtesy of the WPA. Paine has enlarged dramatically since the days of the WPA, with major expansions taking place during World War II, and in 1966 when Boeing chose Everett as the site of its new 747 jetliner assembly plant. Today it is one of the few places where 747s fresh off the assembly line can rub wings with single-engine antiques.

Washington received its first world-class facility in 1949. Seattle-Tacoma International Airport was built at a cost of $11 million, and while only two airlines—Western and Northwest Orient— were using the field, its runways were bustling with a total of 10 scheduled flights each day.

The Grant County Airport at Moses Lake was dedicated on October 8, 1966, billing itself as the largest civilian airport west of the Mississippi after having been the Air Force's first jet training facility in the United States.

Visitors From Russia

In their two visits to Washington, Russian aviators have favored military air bases over civilian airports to set down. In 1929 four Soviet fliers, traveling from Moscow to New York on a goodwill tour, brought their all-metal Tupolev monoplane, the ANT-4, down at Sand Point. Their craft, "Land of the Soviets," stopped briefly at Pearson Field in Vancouver before continuing on its way.

Eight years later a second Soviet crew crossed the North Pole and landed at Pearson on June 20th, completing the first transpolar flight. The plane, an ANT-25, had remained aloft for an astounding 63 hours and 16 minutes. The pilot of that flight, Valeri Chkalov, later confessed that he was afraid civilians would tear his plane apart, as they had done to Lindbergh's legendary "Spirit of St. Louis." He clearly preferred military security to public praise.

The presence of the military in Washington's aviation history extends back to 1904. At Vancouver's Pearson Field the Army lofted two gas observation balloons high into the air. Pearson, still only roughly developed, was later used for training pilots for World War I.

In 1920 King County broke ground for a landing strip at Sand Point. By 1923 a hangar was up and planes were flying in and out. The county deeded Sand Point to the Navy in 1926, and the base became Naval Air Station Seattle, the Northwest headquarters for naval aviation until 1949, when that function was taken over by the newer, more functional NAS Whidbey Island.

Meanwhile, on the other side of the mountains, Spokane was trying to raise $10,000 to beat out Seattle and Tacoma for the first National Guard Observation Squadron in the state. Spokane succeeded, and in 1924 the third National Guard air squadron to be formed in the country moved onto Felts Field.

Coast Guard aviators moved into the state in 1935, establishing an air base at Port Angeles that is active to this day.

World War II precipitated a flurry of military base-building activity. McChord Air Force Base, built in 12 months and dedicated July 1, 1940, soon became the training ground for the 12th Bombardment Group and the 55th Fighter Group —a pair of squadrons prominent in World War II annals. Today the base is the largest in the Air Defense Command.

On Whidbey Island, farmers were uprooted and farm houses hurriedly demolished to make

Top left: The Coast Guard's Port Angeles air base opened in 1935.
Top right: The Navy's presence at Sand Point dates back to 1926.
Above: This Bell P-39 called McChord AFB home during World War II.
Background: The Coast Guard ready for action.

a "temporary" place where Navy patrol aircraft could be rearmed, refueled, and sent on their way. NAS Whidbey Island was commissioned September 21, 1942. Since then, Whidbey has outlived its temporary status, becoming the major naval air station north of San Francisco and west of Chicago.

Larson Air Force Base, five miles from Moses Lake, was activated on November 24, 1942, as another temporary site. Its first task was to train P-38 Lightning pilots and, later, the combat crews for B-17 Flying Fortresses. The facility remained operational until 1965, the testing ground for such advanced craft as the B-47 Stratojet, the B-50, and B-52. Titan I intercontinental ballistic missiles were installed here in the 1960s. When the base was deactivated, the Air Force deeded Larson's well-used airstrip to Grant County.

Below: Pangborn's Bellanca Skyrocket made the first nonstop transpacific flight. Bottom: Nat Browne's Fokker Universal tried a running start to Tokyo. Right: Hugh Herndon and Clyde Pangborn (far right).

Daredevils Pangborn and Herndon

On October 5, 1931, daredevil Clyde "Upside-Down" Pangborn and his navigator Hugh Herndon slid the belly of their Bellanca monoplane "Miss Veedol" along the dirt of the Wenatchee air field. At this point the pair undoubtedly knew that their names would be emblazoned in the annals of Washington aviation. They had just beaten the odds and completed the first nonstop transpacific flight.

Pangborn was a barnstormer nicknamed for his trademark stunt—lazily rolling his Curtiss JN-4D over and flying it upside down. He was a partner in the 1920s with Ivan Gates, proprietor of Gates Flying Circus, the most popular of traveling air shows. In 1926, when passenger travel was in its infancy, Gates' pilots took more than 200,000 paying customers up for a brief tour of the skies. It is said that Pangborn himself ferried that many passengers during his remarkable career.

Pangborn grew up in Brewster, Okanogan County. His mother and brother later moved to Wenatchee and were waiting at the air field when he returned from his record-making flight. Surprisingly, he and Herndon had not set out to be the first nonstop transpacific fliers. In fact, they originally were after the around-the-world speed record. A rash of problems—particularly those associated with Herndon's navigational skills—necessitated the scrubbing of that effort. Rather than return home with nothing to show, they decided to fly from Japan to the United States. The rest, as they say, is Washington history.

The Japanese did not take kindly to the two Americans invading their air space or taking photographs over parts of their country that were off-limits to foreigners. Pangborn and Herndon had to spend two months in a Japanese jail for spying. When they got out, the pair made a bee-line for Sabishiro Beach on Honshu Island, 300 miles from Tokyo, where their airplane awaited.

Shortly after taking off, Pangborn dumped the airplane's 300-pound landing gear. Flying at an average speed of 117 mph, the two men made the historic crossing of the Pacific in 41 hours and 13 minutes. When Pangborn and Herndon landed in Wenatchee, a representative from a Japanese newspaper was there to greet them with a check for $25,000. This sum was only half the prize money that inspired so many transpacific attempts either from or to Washington around 1930.

The other half of the prize money was put up by the Seattle Chamber of Commerce. The Chamber's award, however, had restrictions that made winning it extremely difficult; the flight had to originate either within 50 miles of Tokyo or 10 miles of Seattle. Therefore Pangborn and Herndon were not eligible for the second $25,000. They shared the belief of other aviators of that era that there simply was no runway within 50 miles of Tokyo long enough to start the flight.

Later "Miss Veedol" was cleaned up and sent to Seattle and put on display at the Bon Marche department store. Because Herndon, whose family was wealthy, financed the trip, Pangborn got the glory but not the prize money for his accomplishment.

Nat Browne.

Valiant Attempts

Not everybody was as lucky as Pangborn and Herndon. The route between Washington and Japan was filled with failures.

On August 19, 1929, Harold Bromley rolled his brand new Lockheed monoplane "City of Tacoma" down a ramp at Tacoma's airport. The airplane managed to lift into the air for about 100 yards before its fuel load pulled Bromley back to earth.

In 1932 Nat Browne made his attempt. Browne's theory was that if he could add fuel once he got off the ground, he could get across the Pacific with ease. As soon as Browne was airborne over Puget Sound, he flew underneath Wark's plane to link up and take on his fuel load. No such luck. The hose dangling from Wark's plane hit the tail of Browne's plane and knocked the whole craft to pieces. Browne bailed out and landed in the Sound, suffering minor injuries.

The Seattle Chamber of Commerce never did have to part with its share of the prize money.

The "Spokane Sun God"

On August 15, 1929, Art Walker and Nick Mamer took off from Felts Field in their aircraft, "Spokane Sun God," to begin an epic nonstop, two-way transcontinental flight. Their route would take them from Spokane to New York, a total distance of 7,200 miles. By mission's end, the aviators would log a total of 115 consecutive hours aloft.

In a year when many aviators were attempting endurance records by flying hour after hour over a town or an airport, Walker's and Mamer's effort stood out—not just for the time aloft or the distance covered, but for the valuable information on in-flight refueling it provided.

The biplane's extra load of fuel made the take-off from Felts Field tricky. The crowd that gathered to watch the "Sun God" and its crew attempt to expand the frontiers of aviation cheered as the plane wobbled skyward.

The first in-flight refueling took place over San Francisco. Mamer guided the "Sun God" into position underneath the tanker plane, the "Californian." Soon the fuel line from the "Californian" was whipping back and forth in the wind. Walker, who had pulled on his helmet and goggles, lifted his upper body out of the "Sun God," grabbed the line, and guided it to the fuel tank of his craft.

Walker and Mamer repeated this procedure across the country and back. Unsophisticated as it might sound today, this innovative method was one of the precursors of today's routine in-flight refueling of high-speed military aircraft.

Above left: The "Sun God" set its refueling record in 1929. Below: Nick Mamer (left) and Art Walker—endurance record champs. Above right: Percy Barnes set up his Lakeview aviation school in 1919. Below right: Hundreds got their wings at Lana Kurtzer's Lake Union base.

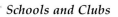

The first flying schools in Washington could turn out pilots fairly quickly, since in those days a mere 10 solo hours earned a flier a license. Percy Barnes was one of the earliest flight instructors, running Barnes Aviation School in Lakeview in 1919. Elliott Merrill took on students at his Washington Aircraft and Transportation Corporation.

Lana Kurtzer founded Kurtzer Flying Service at Boeing Field in 1928 and three years later added a seaplane base on Lake Union. He and his counterpart on the other side of the Cascades, Yakima's Charles D. McAllister, put together two of the longest and most productive flight instructor careers in history.

Washington's first flying clubs were primarily recreational associations—people pooling their resources so they could have an airplane to fly. Today a broad spectrum of special interest groups —small plane owners, glider pilots, retired aircraft workers and others with active interest in aeronautics—meet regularly throughout the state.

After World War I, a group calling itself the "Quiet Birdmen" took wing. Primarily devoted to keeping the great oral tradition of "hangar flying" alive, its members still gather to swap stories about the aviation-associated thrills of yesteryear.

In 1957, the Washington Wing of the OX-5 Club was chartered. OX-5 is a nationwide group whose purpose is to record the history of the development of air transportation, placing special emphasis on the years from 1920 to 1940.

Washington's involvement in aerial warfare was fairly limited during World War I, but that was to change. While Boeing Airplane Company's 21-person work force was kept busy throughout "The Great War" assembling C series trainers and HS2L flying boats for the Navy, it wasn't until "Rosie the Riveter" and her thousands of co-workers went to work at the Boeing factory during World War II that Washington made a significant contribution to a war effort.

Women took on many new roles during the war, and not just in the factories. Barbara Erickson, who was a Boeing inspector, joined the Women's Army Service Pilots in 1942 and became the first woman pilot to receive the Air Medal. Blanche Bross of Ocean Park was one of the first 13 women trained to fly the B-17.

Without a doubt, the B-17 was the workhorse of the American bombing effort. Crews in Seattle finished 16 of these appropriately named "Flying Fortresses" a day at the peak of production in 1943. Then the Boeing factories switched over to producing the B-29, the only plane that could carry out long-range attacks—and could deliver with confidence the newly developed atomic bomb to its top secret targets.

"Pappy" Boyington of Okanogan was the most famous of the fliers this state sent to war. As a Marine Corps commander of the Black Sheep Squadron in the Pacific, he shot down 28 enemy

aircraft. His book *Baa Baa Black Sheep* became a popular television series starring Robert Conrad.

Communities all across Washington bustled with the urgent training of heavy bomber crews between 1942 and 1945. Young fliers from all over the United States came to the Walla Walla Army Air Field to train aboard B-17s and Consolidated B-24 Liberators.

Bases that served as supply and maintenance depots also made major contributions toward ending the war. Fairchild Air Force Base, established at Spokane in 1942, set a record when its crews had overhauled 10,000 engines by June of 1945.

The demands of World War II took airplanes to a point that would not have been dared in peacetime. Operational testing of new models often took place in the air, a hasty practice that led to the death of Boeing's chief test pilot, Eddie Allen. In peacetime, the fire that developed during one test flight of the B-29 bomber would have grounded the airplane that Allen flew. But in his haste to press the B-29 into service, Allen took the prototype out again on February 18, 1943. This time, when fire broke out it quickly spread, causing an explosion that sent the airplane crashing into the nearby Frye meat packing plant. Allen and his 11 crew members were killed, along with 19 Frye employees.

Lovelace Leaps for Life

Not many people would have the confidence to take the leap that Colonel W.R. Lovelace did back in 1943. Lovelace wanted to find out whether or not his oxygen equipment could keep a man alive during the 12 minutes it would take to descend from the stratosphere to breathable air, so he jumped from a B-17 flying at 40,200 feet over eastern Washington. The information he sought would be vital to bomber pilots who would soon be flying in the thin air of high altitudes.

The jump was Lovelace's first, and the first of its kind in history. When the static line pulled his chute open, he watched a leather glove and its silk liner being ripped from his left hand. Then the daring parachutist blacked out, regaining consciousness minutes later on the ground. Slightly battered, Lovelace was living proof that a pilot could indeed bail out in the stratosphere and, with the proper equipment, live to tell about it.

INTERNATIONAL ORGANIZATION
99
WOMEN PILOTS

air mail

Left to right: Members of the prestigious 99 Club proudly wore this patch. • A smile from Pete Bowers in his popular "Fly Baby." • The Seattle Air Mail Baseball Team. • Women fliers receive an achievement award at Boeing Field. • "Hells Angels" and other WWII bombers stopped at Boeing Field. • This Douglas C-124 Globemaster was a regular at McChord AFB. • Amelia Earhart flew Western to visit Seattle in 1934.

Scrapbook

After World War II, prosperity and a lot of surplus airplanes turned people's minds to finding new roles for aviation. Fire patrols over the state's forest lands had begun as early as 1923, when Nick Mamer made regular passes over eastern Washington in a DH-4 on loan to the U.S. Forest Service. Smoke jumpers and borate sprayers were soon added to the forest fire-fighting arsenal during the post-war years. Aerial photography also grew into a sophisticated surveying tool in times of peace. The airplane's use in search-and-rescue missions and as an air ambulance increased.

To some, the opportunities for Washington's versatile aircraft may have appeared endless. For hauling remote ore deposits, why not employ an airborne dump truck? And for logging timber on steep hillsides, how about a helicopter skycrane?

One of the earliest post-war endeavors to focus widespread attention on the potential of industrial aviation was the development of the "Air Tractor." In 1952, Dick Baxter of Yakima's Central Aircraft, a large crop-dusting service using war surplus planes, asked Robert T. Lamson, a former Boeing test pilot, to design a craft specifically for spraying and dusting crops. The high-gap, gull-wing, wood-and-fabric biplane made its first flight late in 1953. Although Central-Lamson built only two prototypes before shutting down its operation due to lack of capital, the Air Tractor made a big impression in Washington and across the country. Aviation magazines touted the potential of the Tractor, while Borden used it to advertise Elmer's Glue. The Duke of Edinburgh even praised it in a speech on the future of aviation!

Above: Smoke jumpers joined the brigade of forest fire fighters in the '40s. Below: This Ford Trimotor conducted experimental smoke jumps over Washington. Background: The 1953 Air Tractor opened up new fields for aviation.

Administrative Organizations

As aviation grew in importance, it developed a strong support network. One of the most significant members of this network is the Federal Aviation Administration, which emerged in 1958 from a myriad of federal regulatory agencies. In Washington, the FAA's main office is at King County Airport. The agency regulates the airways, manages air traffic, and conducts research and development. It is assisted in some of these tasks by the Washington State Department of Transportation's Division of Aeronautics, also headquartered at King County Airport. This body was formed in 1947 and is responsible for coordinating all air search and rescue operations in the state.

The Washington wing of the Civil Air Patrol—the civilian auxiliary of the U.S. Air Force—was chartered in 1941, one of the first in the nation. While its original mission was to patrol the coast, the CAP now runs a cadet training program and does extensive work in aerospace education.

Homebuilt Aircraft

So-called "homebuilts" have a history as long as aviation itself. In fact, in the early days there was little to distinguish airplanes built by hobbyists from those creations of serious experimenters and would-be manufacturers. A resurgence of homebuilding activity occurred after World War II, when federal regulations loosened up to admit an "amateur-built" category of aircraft into the picture. M.B. Taylor of Longview was beginning work on his Aerocar, a vehicle that he believed would turn air transportation even more practical by making it door-to-door. In 1947 he formed Aerocar, Inc., and 23 years later the Ford Motor Company asked the FAA for permission to build 25,000 of Taylor's new Aerocars. According to Mr. Taylor, production was not undertaken, however, because the FAA said it did not want the skies to become freeways full of flying cars.

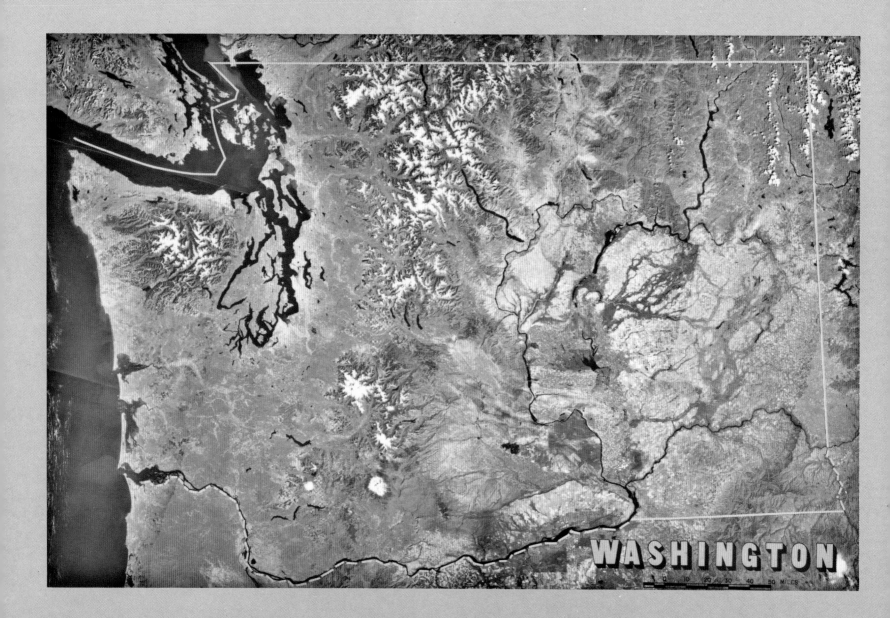

WASHINGTON

New Directions

THREE

Seen From Outer Space

Most of us can only imagine what Washington might look like at a distance of approximately 500 miles. Up to the present time, the majority of far-sighted viewers have not been human but man-made satellites orbiting the Earth and sharing their unique perspectives with technicians far below. Satellites such as these have been in place since the mid-1970s, silently patrolling the fringe of outer space — the ideal vantage point for the objective study of life on Earth.

Like those precious aerial photos of the Alaska-Yukon-Pacific Exposition of 1909, each picture transmitted by satellite — in actuality a mosaic of thousands of individual images assembled into one composite photo — gives us a new perspective on our own lives. A modern Landsat satellite, for example, is capable of transmitting detailed information about landforms no larger than the average suburban lot — information that can be used to predict the weather, create accurate high-quality maps, study patterns of land use, even monitor the movement of icebergs in Antarctica.

These pictures also give us another bit of important information. They tell us how Washington relates to the rest of the world. With its network of mail stations, airports, and military bases firmly in place, it was only a matter of time before Washingtonians would expand the horizons of flight far beyond the borders of the state. Satellite photographs like the one reproduced here show us how Washington is geographically linked to the rest of the country and to the other nations sharing the Pacific.

It may have seemed out of place to Boeing Company customers when the first color pictures of rocket ships, space stations and an unmanned craft called the "Martian Explorer" started showing up in its catalogs and brochures. Nonetheless, as early as 1959 Boeing researchers had made a commitment to solving "the problems associated with hypersonic, orbital, and space vehicles."

To Boeing, this new interest in outer space was a logical extension of existing company goals. As Washington's aeronautical designers continued to break the last remaining barriers to manned flight, where would the final design frontier be found if not in the far reaches of space?

The U.S. government more than agreed with this line of reasoning. Recognizing Boeing's past record, in 1961 it awarded the ever-expanding company with a contract to design, build, and test the first-stage booster of the giant Apollo/Saturn V moon rocket. Other contracts from the National Aeronautics and Space Administration (NASA) soon followed. Current projects include the design and construction of living quarters, laboratories, and logistics modules for NASA's latest effort—a space station whose launch date has been scheduled for 1994.

Aerospace contracts have also been awarded in recent years to Washington-based companies such as Redmond's Microsoft Corporation and the John Fluke Manufacturing Company of Everett. As the first one hundred years of flight in the state draw to a close, Washington's flight engineers and research technicians will be shaping the next one hundred years of our nation's outer space programs.

Right: A shuttle comes to rest in this artist's rendering of a space station docking exercise. Below: LANDSAT satellites like this one keep tabs on our state from afar. Below middle: Important flight experiments are conducted in the wind tunnel at the University of Washington. Below right: Phil Church joined the UW faculty in 1935 and founded the Department of Atmospheric Sciences.

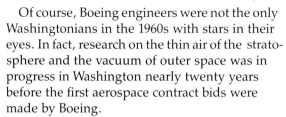

Of course, Boeing engineers were not the only Washingtonians in the 1960s with stars in their eyes. In fact, research on the thin air of the stratosphere and the vacuum of outer space was in progress in Washington nearly twenty years before the first aerospace contract bids were made by Boeing.

In 1947 Phil E. Church was appointed Chairman of the University of Washington's Department of Climatology, which was later renamed the Department of Atmospheric Sciences. Church's appointment initiated the university's active role in atmospheric and meteorological research. Faculty and students are presently engaged in such lofty pursuits as the investigation of cosmic radiation and remote sensing from space.

A second university program, the Department of Aeronautics and Astronomics, offers undergraduate and advanced degrees in engineering science, placing emphasis on what the departmental catalog calls "the design and development of vehicles operating within the atmosphere of space."

At military air bases like Fairchild AFB and NAS Whidbey Island, and at Boeing's Advanced Systems Company in Seattle, research in strategic air defense is ongoing. While many of these top-secret projects are kept cloistered away from public view, some of the more visible products of this highly specialized line have included the Airborne Warning and Control System and the V-22 Osprey, a tilt-rotor aircraft that can take off and land like a helicopter as well as travel at speeds and distances ordinarily associated with modern turboprop airplanes.

Tex Johnston

A.M. "Tex" Johnston could have easily earned a place in Washington's flight history based on his professional record alone. One of the state's top test pilots, he played a major role in the development of Boeing's B-52 and 700 series of aircraft. However, thanks to a single crowd-pleasing stunt, Johnston's professional record may have been eclipsed by his popular acclaim.

On August 7, 1955, the flamboyant, 40-year-old pilot was asked to put the company's brand-new 707 prototype through its paces following a performance of the Blue Angels precision flight team at Seattle's Seafair festival. To the shock of Boeing executives and the delight of the 250,000 fairgoers on hand that afternoon, Johnston did just that— executing a couple of leisurely barrel rolls above the lake. The stunt drew cheers from the crowd, and as some tell it, caused Boeing president William Allen to turn to his seatmate, who had heart trouble, and exclaim, "Give me about 10 of your heart pills!"

Advances in aviation, largely from the Boeing Company's western Washington plants, have enabled the state to meet the growing demands of both domestic and world markets. No longer the isolated "upper left-hand corner" of the country, Washington's airborne trade routes give its manufacturers and merchants the chance to share the wealth of the state with other parts of the country as well as with the nations of the Pacific Rim.

Each year more national and international passenger carriers— United, Northwest, American, Delta, Japan, and Thai International to name just a few—are adding Washington to their lists of scheduled stops. Others like Alaska Airlines and Horizon have clearly chosen to base their operations out of Washington.

Washington importers have also benefitted greatly from the increased cargo-carrying capacity of dependable, modern airplanes like the Boeing 747. As Washington continues to build upon its role as a major port of entry on the West Coast, more freight companies are favoring airport hangars over traditional waterfront docks to unload their valuable cargo.

Global trade is a two-way street, evident in the increased interest in our regional products expressed by merchants from abroad. Of course, at the top of these regional products stands the commercial jetliner. The Boeing Company has forecasted an estimated $222 billion in airplane deliveries—many to Latin America and countries of the Pacific Rim—by the year 2000.

Washington is a popular destination for visitors from around the world.

Advances in Aircraft

In 1952 the Boeing Company announced it would invest $16 million to build a prototype of an entirely new jet-powered transport airplane. Two years later this prototype, the 367-80, dramatically challenged the carrying and distance capacities of all previous transport designs. Production versions of this new jet were called 707s. Subsequent members of the 700 family have contributed even more to Washington's position of power in world trade and transportation.

Boeing matched the success of the 707 with its 720 and 720B, a pair of lighter-weight, shorter-bodied aircraft designed to travel the shorter air routes of the world. United Airlines became the first buyer of the 720 in November 1957.

Next came the Boeing 727-100 and 727-200. Both jets would replace the many short- to medium-range piston and turboprop airplanes still in service in the early 1960s. Both were remarkably well-received.

The Boeing 737-100, -200, -300, and -400 are short-range airplanes designed to complement the larger members of the 700 family. The first of the 737s took to the skies in April 1967.

The Boeing 747 is affectionately known as a giant jetliner—a 231-foot-long airplane with an awesome 195-foot wingspan.

The Boeing 757 and 767 Twinjets are fuel-efficient, short-to-medium-range jetliners that were test flown in 1982 and 1981 respectively. They are popular with pilots and passengers alike.

Left to right: NASA contracts have kept Washington strong. • Passengers on this flight have a great view of Mt. Rainier. • A hold full of cargo. • It's hard to mistake the distinctive AWACS silhouette. • Boeing's Red Barn being moved to the site of the Museum of Flight. • A Boeing-built moon buggy far from its Washington home. • A bilingual direction sign aids international visitors.

Baggage Claim
手荷物引渡し所
Ticketing
航空券発賣カウンター

Scrapbook

Test pilot Edmund T. Allen.

Pathfinders

In recognition of its commitment to keeping the Northwest's flight heritage alive, each year the Museum of Flight identifies as many as five people who have made significant contributions to aerospace development in the Northwest. To date, more than 30 recipients of the Museum's coveted Pathfinder Award have been named. A substantial percentage of these individuals singled out for recognition were born in Washington State or based their aviation careers here.

Prominent Washington Pathfinders include: Edmund T. Allen, William M. Allen, William E. Boeing, Harl V. Brackin, Fred S. Eastman, Clairmont L. Egtvedt, Thomas Hamilton, Eddie Hubbard, Phillip G. Johnson, A.M. Johnston, Frederick K. Kirsten, Nicholas B. Mamer, Louis Marsh, George C. Martin, A. Elliot Merrill, Charles N. Montieth, Clyde Pangborn, Maynard L. Pennell, George S. Schairer, Clayton Scott, George Stoner, Leslie R. Tower, and Edward C. Wells.

Above: The Museum of Flight's Great Gallery opened in 1987. Below: Colorful exhibits at the Museum of Flight include more than 30 full-size aircraft. Right: The supersonic jet airliner Concorde touched down in November 1984 behind the Museum of Flight, which, at that time, consisted only of the Red Barn.

With so much interest and activity in aviation centered in Washington, it may have seemed inevitable to some that one of the West Coast's largest flight museums would be located here. However, it took almost 20 years of groundwork before one group of visionary air enthusiasts could bring such a facility to Seattle. In 1965 the freshly formed foundation set to work, salvaging a rare 1929 Model 80-A airliner and restoring another Boeing craft, the Model 247 D, even before its members had secured a permanent space to display their treasures. Eleven years later, the foundation found a perfect home—the original Red Barn factory used by the fledgling Boeing Airplane Company, sitting in disuse near the shores of the Duwamish Waterway. After intense negotiation with the city, the county, and the Port of Seattle, the foundation was able to acquire the dilapidated, but historic structure and to move it to the south end of King County Airport.

Restoration of the Red Barn was completed in 1983, marking the first phase of an extensive two-part program to build a world-class air and space museum. Exhibits in the Red Barn trace flight history from its earliest origins through 1938, relying heavily on the wood frame setting of the old Boeing Airplane Company to give a feeling of these pioneering times in aviation.

In the meantime, the Pacific Northwest Aviation Historical Foundation proudly renamed itself the Museum of Flight Foundation. The Museum's long-awaited second phase, an architectural triumph in glass and steel called the Great Gallery, opened in 1987. Now assembled within the Great

Gallery's three million cubic feet of usable space are aircraft—many from Washington's colorful past—representing significant eras of aviation history. Through an array of imaginative signs, interactive components, and specially selected artifacts, the Museum of Flight is able to share with visitors the many stories surrounding each aspect of manned flight.

But as important as the Museum's impressive collection of airplanes are its programs—everything from public appearances by guest lecturers such as "Wrong Way" Corrigan or Brigadier General Robert Lee Scott, Jr., to such activities as the popular "Make It and Take It" workshops offered each weekend for younger visitors.

Wings Still Aloft

This book has offered many views of Washington and its 100-year history. We've surveyed the state from a balloon tenuously tethered 500 feet above Seattle's Alaska-Yukon Pacific Exposition. We've seen it from an airplane racing across the Inland Empire at the completion of Spokane's National Air Races of 1927, and glimpsed it via remote sensing satellite from a distance of over 500 miles.

Of course, none of these dramatically different perspectives of Washington could have possibly been formed were it not for the state's enthusiasm for aviation back in the 1880s. Washington's 100-year love affair with flight, and her firm commitment to research and experimentation, has made for an exciting story too rich to successfully chronicle even in the most comprehensive and scholarly treatment of regional flight history.

Wings Over Washington *is a story that could best be told by many thousands of bold innovators and explorers. Whether they know it or not, Washington's pilots, her ground crews, instructors, fabricators, technicians, and passengers have had a major hand in shaping the identity and economy of the state, and it will be fascinating to see how these same individuals and their new recruits will affect global aviation history over the next 100 years.*